LEOPARDS

Cyndi Gamble & Rodney Griffiths

Colin Baxter Photography, Grantown-on-Spey, Scotland

LEOPARDS

The WorldLife Library

Written by leading naturalists and illustrated by the world's top photographers

First published in Great Britain in 2004 by
Colin Baxter Photography Ltd
Grantown-on-Spey
PH26 3NA
Scotland

www.worldlifelibrary.co.uk

Text by Cyndi Gamble © 2004 Rodney Griffiths

Photographs © 2004 Rodney Griffiths

WorldLife Library Series

A CIP Catalogue record for this book is available from the British Library.

ISBN 1-84107-254-0

Printed in China

(m) 599.7x423 G

Contents

Both parents of this young black male leopard have
passed on to it the recessive melanism gene. Its twin was spotted, so it must
have received a dominant spotted gene from at least one parent.

Natural History of Leopards

Of the 36 species in the cat family, three (the leopard, the snow leopard and the clouded leopard) are what we commonly refer to as leopards. This is where the confusion begins. There is another species of cat, a small and delicate wild cat, found in Asia, that is called a leopard cat, but this is not a leopard; it is a small cat whose fur pattern is somewhat leopard-like. The distinctive features of a leopard's coat pattern are the 'rosettes'. But rosettes are also found on the jaguar and these too are sometimes mistaken for leopards. Jaguars are found only in South and Central America while leopards are Old World cats. Jaguar markings have a distinctive spot in the center of their rosette, while leopard rosettes consist of clusters of spots surrounding a darker patch of fur, with no spot in the center.

To confuse the issue even further, in both the leopard and the jaguar there exists a recessive gene that can give rise to a wholly black-colored coat. This is known as melanism. People usually refer to a large black cat as a black panther and assume that it is a separate species; it is not. It is either a melanistic leopard or a melanistic jaguar. In Asia there are black leopards and in The Americas there are black jaguars.

The black leopard is still a spotted leopard and has spots that are indiscernible in most conditions except for bright sunlight. Usually one parent of a melanistic leopard is black, and one parent is spotted. They can have a litter with both spotted and black cubs. Melanism is most frequent in leopard populations found in the tropical regions of Asia. Deep in the tropical jungles it is very dark under the canopy of trees, so a black leopard is well camouflaged with its dark coat. A melanistic leopard would not be found on the open plains of Africa because it would be too conspicuous in the golden grasses, reducing its hunting success to a level that would make survival unviable. Survival for each cat species is dependent on the perfect camouflage. All the markings, whether spots, stripes, or plain coats, are designed to help the feline blend in with its surroundings. The hunter must be able to move slowly toward its prey, inch by inch, so that the prey is barely aware of its presence. Eyes can play tricks in the slowly shifting leaves and grasses. The dark and light of the vegetation blend perfectly with the dark and light coat of a hungry leopard.

The classification of wild cats is an ongoing endeavor. Almost every decade seems to unearth a new way of connecting or separating one species from another. Most of us are unaware that there are 36 different species of wild cats, let alone more than 200 sub-species. In the late nineteenth and early twentieth centuries it was not uncommon for biologists to collect specimens and have sub-species named after themselves. It was the way to get your name recognized in a new growing field. Exploration was the passion of the day, and although many species were known locally, little had been recorded by the scientific world.

The leopard, being the most widespread and diversified of all of the Old World cats, was an obvious target for many a budding biologist out to make a name for themselves. Every book and every generation seemed to record a different number of sub-species. Early biologists based many of their decisions upon taxonomic differences of coat pattern or color, as well as teeth, skull and other anatomical measurements. These differences were visually discernible in an age lacking our sophisticated modern analytical tools.

It has often been a problem for scientists to agree on the number of species there are in the cat family, let alone sub-species. Many list 36 species of cats, but others 37 or even 38 if you include the domestic cat. Biologist Leyhausen established a list in 1979 that had 41 species, but the current taxonomy in use is by Wozencroft in 1993, acknowledging 36 species. But controversy will always exist. For example, there is one unusual cat, called the onza, reputedly to be found in Mexico. It looks like the puma, except more slender, with non-retractable claws similar to the cheetah. A specimen did exist and early writings describe it, but when or if this rare cat will ever be recognized remains uncertain.

The larger cat species at the top of the food chain, the lion, leopard and cheetah, have

been studied the most, since they are easily observed and photographed on the open plains of Africa. They are economically valuable, earning revenue from eco-tourists and hunters. The smaller species are a lot less frequently studied, with their secretive ways deep in the tangle of impenetrable forests, and negligible economic value. In many cases, such as the kodkod and the bay cat, there are only frozen or minimal captive specimens. Others argue that certain species are actually sub-species; some consider the remote Japanese island cat, the Iriomote cat, a sub-species of the leopard cat. Providing a definitive answer is difficult because numbers are so low – is it just one of many sub-species of the leopard cat disappearing or is it one of the most endangered cat species in the world?

But why all the fuss over sub-species and genetic identification? For an animal to be afforded legal protection, it must be firstly defined scientifically. In the battle to save a species, it is important that we have a definition of each wild leopard population since many international wildlife trafficking cases end up in court. Unless the courts can prove beyond a shadow of doubt where a leopard pelt originated from, the case may be very weak. Is it from a leopard that is afforded protection in the wild – or is it from a leopard that was legally hunted in Africa?

Traffickers in wildlife products have sophisticated methods for exploiting legal loopholes. Paperwork can be forged and shipments mislabeled. At many ports it may be easy to deceive customs officers who are not species experts. Until not long ago, those involved in wildlife crimes had an excellent chance of getting away with killing animals unless they were actually caught red-handed. After a crime has been committed, animal products can be radically altered by a tanning or dyeing process, or cut up and merged with other wildlife specimens.

In the new field of wildlife forensics, many disciplines are merging, enabling the collection and evaluation of evidence for legal proceedings in animal crimes. The disciplines of serology, pathology, morphology and DNA fingerprinting are combined to fight the

trafficking of animal parts and products. Although a fairly new science, we are finally doing for animal victims what has been done for humans: solving thousands of crimes with state-of-the-art analysis using genetics and chemistry.

Now the odds are less and less in the criminals' favor. In animal crimes, witnesses are rare. The challenge for scientists is to prove whether an animal pelt came from a protected species or not. To win a case, a prosecutor must be able to distinguish between two sub-species in a way that will hold up under scrutiny in a court of law. Some species can be distinguished with visual analysis but more and more frequently DNA testing is necessary. In human crimes, DNA analysis can give clues to the perpetrator of the crime. In animal crimes, DNA evidence found in a single strand of hair can identify the victim's species, place of origin and hence conservation and protection status. Unfortunately, many animal genomes have not been as well documented as their human counterparts. Groundwork still needs to be done in gathering databases on many species and sub-species. Hopefully, the emerging field of wildlife forensics is making it easier to catch wildlife traffickers involved in the world's estimated seven-billion-dollar annual trade in illegal animal products.

Understanding and utilizing recent knowledge of genetics is useful to man in many other sciences. If you look at cats and humans in terms of their genetic code, we are in fact amazingly alike. In studying the effects of the feline leukemia virus in cats, man has been able to learn more about how cancer cells work. Cats share many of the same genes as humans, so knowledge of how they deal with deadly diseases can help man design drugs and treatments to fight many emerging viruses.

Not only will we be able to fight viruses that plague man, but also those that plague cats. Feline immuno-deficiency virus (FIV) causes death in domestic cats. Medical researchers wondered why it had not spread to wild cats, given that many are exposed to feral cats. Wild cat species that have been studied were found to carry the antibodies to FIV, proving they had been exposed. What prevented the wild population from massive outbreaks of this deadly disease? Explanations could be that the virus may have changed over generations or that the genes within the cats themselves developed to protect their descendants.

Understanding the evolutionary path of the disease and the cat will help scientists protect wild cats in the future. With shrinking populations, many felines will be very susceptible to any new viruses. As cats in the wild enable us to glean many exciting new insights, perhaps helping them survive will coincidentally show us how to sustain a viable environment for ourselves.

The evolution of these perfect hunters remains controversial as there are many gaps in the fossil records and lack of complete skeletons. The ancestors of today's leopard originated about two million years ago in the Indian region. From there they spread to Europe and across Asia. As glaciers moved back and forth across the continents, various populations of leopards became isolated and evolved separate lines. Their basic structure though has not changed for millions of years. The leopard managed to get it right the first time.

Over the eons geographically separated populations would undergo subtle changes to adapt to suit their environment, leading to recognizable sub-species. Today there exists a generally accepted list of 24 sub-species for the leopard. However, recent DNA analysis has shown that many are not as distinct genetically as originally believed and in time we may see a merging to create a new list of only eight sub-species, viz;

Scientific name	Location	Scientific name	Location
Panthera pardus pardus	Africa	*Panthera pardus melas*	Java
Panthera pardus orientalis	Russia, China, Korea	*Panthera pardus delacouri*	South China
Panthera pardus kotiya	Sri Lanka	*Panthera pardus saxicolor*	Persia
Panthera pardus japonensis	North China	*Panthera pardus fusca*	India

At one time, there were 30 different sub-species of leopard in Africa, mostly judged on geographical location and differences in coat pattern. Leopards that lived on the open plains had lighter coats; leopards in the deep jungles had darker coats with more distinctive rosettes. Although adaptations had taken place, genetically there is little difference. Today all African leopards are considered one species, *Panthera pardus pardus*.

When we think about animals being endangered or becoming extinct in the wild, we are usually referring to the species as a whole, but although a particular species may not be endangered, some of its sub-species may be. In the case of the leopard, several of the sub-species are already considered to have become extinct. These include *Panthera pardus adersi* the leopard of the spice island of Zanzibar, *Panthera pardus ciscaucasia* that roamed the Caucasus Mountains between the Black and the Caspian Seas and *Panthera pardus jarvisi* that was found along the Sinai Peninsula from Israel to Turkey. All are lost for ever.

Genetic variation is essential to the long-term adaptability of populations by providing different options in which natural selection can operate. Exotic cats must have diversity in order to respond to expected future environmental change, which includes natural habitat depletion and alteration. New parasites and diseases would develop as habitat is altered. And subsequently, confronted by a new array of problems, a species must adapt or die. Scientists had thought that, in the future, they could re-introduce from captive stock. However, cats kept in a sterile zoo environment will be difficult to re-introduce into a habitat that has changed from when their gene pool entered the zoo world. Only so much genetic diversity can be maintained in the zoo system. Unfortunately, with limited space, many zoos do not have a representative for each cat species, let alone sub-species. Therefore the diversity in the gene pool of many captive felines is being compromised. Presently, there are no breeding pairs for many of the smaller cats, nor for some of the rare sub-species of the bigger cats. As the habitats and the gene pools of many wild cats shrink, it will become increasingly important for biologists to know the genetic relatedness of each species and sub-species in order to manage more intensely the genetic diversity needed for future survival.

Another beautiful leopard sub-species soon destined for extinction in the wild is the Amur, *Panthera pardus orientalis*. It once had a wide range in the far east of Russia, to northeastern China along the Amur and Ussuri River valleys. It was also found in Manchuria and Korea. Thus it is often called a Manchurian or Korean leopard. The Amur leopard also lives farther north than any other leopard sub-species. The area is blanketed in a deciduous forest, so the leopard has a dark orange background color with large rosettes widely spaced with thick borders, to help it blend in. Long legs are an adaptation for walking in the area's deep winter snow. There are fewer than 30 believed to be left in the wild, and there is a limited gene pool in captivity, because of only nine founding members. One of the original members was also believed to be a cross between two sub-species and therefore further diluted the gene pool.

Perhaps the most impressive of the leopard sub-species is the Persian, *Panthera pardus saxicolor*. It is the largest of all the leopards, with a massive, squarish head, looking a little like a spotted lioness. This sub-species is now extinct in the wild and its survival depends upon the 70 or so breeding pairs in captivity around the world.

Genetically, the snow leopard and clouded leopard are two very distinct cats, much different from the leopard. Although they are both in the *Panthera* lineage, they are not in the *Panthera* genus. The four cats in the *Panthera* genus are capable of roaring; the lion, tiger, jaguar, and leopard. The snow leopard and the clouded leopard cannot roar. Genetically they have many differences from the leopard to give them both their own unique genus. Originally the snow leopard was in the same genus as *Panthera uncia*, but recently has been re-classified to its own status of *Uncia uncia*. The clouded leopard, *Neofelis nebulosa*, has always been in a class by itself.

Leopards, like this one in Kenya's Samburu National Reserve, like to rest draped over a tree branch with a clear view of any potential prey that may wander into sight.

*Leopards are formidable climbers – strong neck and chest muscles allow
them to haul their kills up into trees, safe from other predators.*

The Leopard

Characteristics

The leopard is perfection in natural design; sleek, smart, and full of power. It is a compact predator, much smaller than the lion, tiger, or jaguar, the other members of the *Panthera* genus. Capable of amazing physical prowess, the leopard, *Panthera pardus*, is a formidable predator, able to bring down prey significantly larger than itself.

The leopard is the most numerous and adaptable of all the big cats and inhabits just about every environment: desert, mountain, forest, reed bed, bamboo thicket, and cultivated land. Whether it is pine forest, Mediterranean scrub, or rugged foothills, all are suitable habitats for the versatile leopard. Their geographic range extends from Africa through the Middle East, over to India, and China; north to southern Siberia, and south through the Malay Peninsula to the islands of Borneo, Sumatra, and Java. They are the most widespread of all the big cats and are the only species occupying both rainforest and arid desert habitat. The leopard can live without water for periods of time, obtaining its moisture requirements from its prey; however it cannot exist permanently in true desert.

Although the leopard has the smallest body size of the four cats in the *Panthera* group, it is still capable of taking large prey. Its skull is large, giving ample room for the attachment of powerful jaw muscles. Its scapula or shoulder blade is narrow yet broad where muscles attach for climbing. Powerful muscles raise the thorax or chest, enhancing its ability to climb trees. This gives the leopard the ability to not only climb but to lift heavy prey up into a tree. The leopard likes to drape its prey over a limb, to keep it away from other carnivores that would readily steal its meal if left on the ground.

The leopard is a solitary animal that, apart for a brief meeting for mating, stays alone all of its life, so it is essential that it remains free of any injury that could impact its hunting ability. If a leopard cannot hunt it will starve; unlike the lion, which can share the kills of the rest of the pride until it recovers. So, if a feeding leopard is discovered by lions, hyenas or wild dogs, it will sacrifice its meal rather than risk confrontation. The leopard's solitary instinct even exists between mother and cubs. When she feeds at a kill she will not allow her cubs to feed with her. Once she has had her fill she will then move aside to let the cubs feed alone.

With a confusion of spots and rosettes on its face, chest, and legs, the leopard is a perfectly camouflaged predator. Rosettes on the body and flanks, spots on the head, chest, and legs, and rings on the tail, enable it to blend into the dappled light of its habitat. Spots on the muzzle and their position are as varied as each human fingerprint and spots around the muzzle are not symmetrical either. The forehead and chest spots can also form discernible patterns of circles and ovals, or form a necklace or collar. The facial markings vary enough between individual leopards that they can be distinguished from one another, providing useful identification for field biologists studying several leopards and their movements.

Cats have acute hearing, but it is their eyes that surpass those of all others, except raptors, in their ability. In proportion to its body size, the leopard's eyes are actually bigger than ours and more spherical. The lenses are set nearer to the center, giving the cat a wider view. Their peripheral vision is about 280 degrees, whereas we have only 180 degrees. Some prey will freeze when a leopard walks by, but it can catch the slightest movement out of the corner of its eye, perhaps desperate prey trying for a last-minute escape.

The iris of the cat's eye opens and closes to a greater extent than ours, too, allowing more light to enter. The retina, consisting of a combination of rods for light acuity and cones for color, allows the cat to see well in the dark. With more rods and few cones, the cat has sacrificed color awareness to have excellent night vision. This is the cat's greatest asset,enabling it to see much better than humans in the dark. When a cat is chasing prey, it doesn't care what color the prey is; it is more concerned with distance and depth of field.

Keeping a sharp eye on the prey, which is trying desperately to out-maneuver it, the cat must perfectly time when to reach out and snatch it.

The other advantage of the cat's eye is the *tapetum lucidum*, a layer of cells backing the retina. These cells form a reflective surface from which any light not absorbed on its passage through the eye is bounced back to give a second pass to the light-sensitive cells within the retina. This leads to the eerie glowing eye shine that cats have when we see them in the dark. If you have ever witnessed this glow you can understand why primitive man thought the cat possessed magical powers.

Not only is the stare of a cat in the dark frightening; many who have experienced the powerful stare of the leopard in the daylight, automatically feel like prey. The leopard's expression is always the same, whether you are dealing with a wild or captive leopard. They are invariably calculating their next move. This gripping expression telegraphs to us that we are potential food. Hidden behind a mantle of spots is an animal whose appetite has not changed much in thousands of years. Man is an easy target for a hungry leopard.

Early hominids were thought to have scavenged prey from leopard and lion kills, which put them in dangerous proximity to a predator possessive of his food. Even today, leopards also still look to man for an easy meal. Dinner is served in the form of slow-moving sheep and cattle. Although guarded by man, the leopard is clever enough to attack at night, when humans sleep, or perhaps during a rainy spell when in their huts keeping dry. A simple corral does nothing to stop the leopard, but merely places all its food in one large serving bowl. This can lead to the leopard killing more than it really needs to survive. When panic sets in, it's easy for a predator to get caught up in the moment.

Many believe the drive for food is the strongest and consumes every waking moment of a carnivore's life. Others believe there is also a separate drive to kill, which is equally as strong. Is it purely for the fact that it can kill, or is it so instinctive that the cat cannot help but kill?

Colonel Jim Corbett was a famous hunter in the early 1900s who spent a lifetime in India hunting man-eating tigers and leopards. Successful for being able to stalk leopards that had become man-eaters, he was not easily fooled by them, as were others. Although the leopard started out being the hunted, it easily turned the tables and became the hunter. Corbett considered the leopard one of the strongest and most intelligent of all wild animals. Two man-eating leopards in Kumaon, India, had killed 525 people before being shot by Corbett. The cats had developed a taste for human flesh; he believed that this was acquired after major epidemics, typical in that time and place, had wiped out many people, creating opportunities for leopards to dine on human corpses.

The leopard kills its prey by a suffocating grip on the windpipe. South Luangwa National Park, Zambia.

But leopards can dine on much more than just humans. Because they are found in such a wide variety of locations across Africa, the Middle East, Asia, and north to Siberia, the leopard has one of the most varied diets of all the felines. Humans are found everywhere, whereas other prey they rely on for sustenance are indigenous to only certain areas: young pandas and bamboo rats are taken in China, hog deer in Nepal, langur in India, moufflon sheep in the Caucasus Mountains, and rain forest duykers in Central Africa. This ability to adapt and eat a very broad diet means the leopard consumes everything from a large dung beetle to an adult eland.

The preferred prey is small to medium ungulates such as muntjac, roe and chital deer,

mountain goat, tufted deer, ibex, markhor, turkmenian sheep, impala and gazelles. They also go after smaller prey, such as rock hyrax, porcupine, wild goat, pig, partridge, primates, and even fish. In the never-ending quest for food, the leopard daily walks its territory along familiar trails, ridges, and near watering holes. It's a creature of habit, scent-marking the same tree or rock, visiting the same game trails and watching the same prey herds, each dependent on the other; the leopard needing the prey for food, the prey needing the leopard to keep the herd strong, by culling the weak, sick, and genetically inferior.

With a territory ranging from 5 to 50 square miles (13 to 130 sq km), depending on prey availability, a male leopard is always ready to defend his home from intruders. Some intruders are tolerated if they are female. The territory of several female leopards will overlap that of a single male. Most of the year they will avoid each other, leaving only scent marks to indicate their passing. Only when the female is in estrus will the male become interested in his close neighbor. The initial courtship may start with frequent scent marking and vocal communication. The female will call into the night, 'Where are you?' she wants to know. 'Over here', is his response.

The leopard is one of the four big cats (*Panthera* genus) called the 'Great Cats' that are capable of roaring. All of these cats have a long elastic ligament, rather than solid bone, connected to the hyoid apparatus in the throat. The hyoid determines whether a cat roars or purrs. This ligament is largest in the lion, approximately 6 in (15 cm) long, but stretching to 8 or 9 inches (20 or 23 cm). The roar of the leopard is nothing like the roar of the mighty lion. It does not resonate nearly as loudly, and seems to consist of shorter bursts of breath. Although a diminutive roar compared to that of the lion, it is still information on territory and breeding status critical to the leopard.

Once the male and female find each other, their courtship is brief. After mating, the male

Leopards will snarl to intimidate each other but will rarely risk a fight.

is off again, never to raise his young. Leopards reproduce slowly, having two to three cubs on average once every couple of years. That is because they stay with their mother until 12 to 18 months of age. Only if her cubs are lost or killed will she reproduce sooner. Since they are small and helpless, the mother will frequently move her cubs, so their scent will not give away their hiding place to other predators. The female will spend her time in a smaller area of her territory until the cubs are older. They develop quickly in order to survive. They are capable of racing up the nearest tree, or diving into a narrow rock crevice, which is their only protection from lions, hyenas, or wild dogs. The female will start ranging further away from her cubs, when they are able to fend for themselves. She can be gone for 24 hours or more to hunt. Being alert and agile at a young age is an important survival skill for a leopard.

As soon as cubs open their eyes, they see everything in the world as something to pounce on. They stalk and pounce each other, their mother, and anything blowing in the wind. The hunting strategy of the cat is basically the same, whether it is a domestic cat or a large lion. One strategy is to be mobile, always moving towards the prey, searching the creek beds and rock crevices until a potential prey animal is encountered. The second strategy is to remain stationary, and the cats are masters at being stationary for long periods of time. They barely move a whisker, waiting patiently near game trails and watering holes until an animal comes along. Once potential prey is found, most cats crouch and approach to the nearest available cover in a low slinking position. When they are close, they stop and watch, lying snug to the ground. Whiskers are spread wide like tentacles, and ears face forward. To prepare for the chase, they push back on their hind legs, like a sprinter into a starting block. When the moment is right, they will dart forward in a low run in an attempt to catch the prey.

A leopard cub left hidden in a rocky outcrop by its mother while she goes off to hunt.

It seems the cat would have the advantage, but the prey is not without its advantages. Zigging and zagging, turning on an instant, they try to outmaneuver their pursuer. Most times they are successful. Cats are lucky to catch their prey once out of every 15 or 20 attempts. Odds are in favor of the prey species, especially against a young inexperienced leopard. Cats must be taught how to hunt by their mother. First, she will bring live prey back to the den area, and release it near her cubs so they can practice their skills. Although chasing and pouncing come naturally, she must show them the throat grip used to suffocate their prey. Later, when they are as big as her, they are still dependent on her hunting skills. It will take years of learning the coordination and timing needed to reach her level. These predatory skills have evolved over many centuries to create the perfect predator.

On the Brink

The leopard lived side by side with man for centuries, helping him develop his hunting and survival skills. With primitive clubs and snare traps, only the bravest warrior took on the crafty leopard. In early times, there was tremendous power and prestige if one was able to kill a leopard.

To this day Zulu chiefs still wear leopard skins to show their status. It was not until the advent of guns that leopard numbers became threatened. Any man could now easily kill a leopard by hiding in a blind or shooting from a safe distance. Soon a trade in leopard pelts developed, and reached a peak in the 1960s and 70s, with as many as 60,000 sold per year. Finally in 1975, the leopard was listed as endangered by CITES, the Convention on International Trade in Endangered Species.

Despite the leopard's problem with man, it still lives easily around villages. There are even reports of their presence near major cities. These astounding creatures seem to be

A Zulu chief wears his badge of office – a leopard skin.

able to conform and cope in close proximity to human settlements. Many regions must deal with problem leopards in and around people and livestock. Villagers resent international interference when their livestock and livelihood are at risk. If the wild ungulate prey the leopard depends on is depleted, it is forced to turn to livestock or starve. Unfortunately, their natural prey is eliminated for man's food, or to make grazing room for his domestic livestock. Much of the livestock is roaming free, so it is hard for a carnivore to see the distinction between their natural food, and food that belongs to man.

Still the leopard has fared better than any of the other big cats. In some areas once occupied by lions, tigers, or cheetahs, only the leopard remains.

Whether man eliminated the predator, or the predator's prey and habitat, he thought there was an endless supply of both. For many years, zoos and wildlife collections were easily re-stocked from the wild. Man had little knowledge of disease, diet, or breeding conditions necessary to maintain a healthy captive population. It was simply a matter of organizing an expedition to collect more. It wasn't until it was almost too late for some species that man became aware that there was not a limitless supply of animals in the wild. The early Romans were responsible for eliminating lions from many parts of Africa and the Middle East, so great was their demand for them in the coliseums. Maharajahs and sultans had the same effect on the Indian cheetah, collected in great numbers for sport hunting. Leopards in the most populated regions became extinct because man eliminated their prey.

No matter what the reason, man has had to learn about wild animal husbandry, with wildlife populations diminishing or disappearing. Medication for diseases, special diets for nutrition, and natural enclosures for successful breeding have all been developed to create healthier populations of wild animals in captivity. Today our knowledge of captive animals is critical to maintaining many species that are rapidly becoming extinct in the wild.

Slinking low, this leopard is stalking a warthog in Botswana's Okavango Delta.

(2,590,000 sq km) area in 12 ethnically diverse countries: Afghanistan, Bhutan, China, India, Kazakstan, Kyrgyz Republic, Mongolia, Nepal, Pakistan, Russia, Tajikistan and Uzbekistan.

The snow leopard's body is superbly designed for mountain predation. It has large snowshoe-like paws, short thick legs and well-developed chest muscles to aid in climbing steep mountain ledges. Its skull is flat across the top, with a deep notch down to a wide nose, allowing for larger nasal passages to breathe in the thin, cold mountain air. The snow leopard has the longest, thickest tail of all the cats, vital for balancing as it races up narrow game trails after its sure-footed prey, the mountain sheep and goats. The snow leopard stalks prey that is every bit as elusive and at home in the mountains as it is. Favorite prey include the legendary Marco Polo sheep, with one of the longest curled horns in the world; the markhor, with long spiralled horns; the ibex; Himalayan tahr, bharal sheep and several varieties of deer. However, the snow leopard is an opportunistic hunter who will also eat smaller gazelles, rabbit, marmot, and even the tiny pika.

Following the migration of their larger prey along the ridgelines, bluffs and cliffs can make eating a major uncertainty at times. Unfortunately, many of the exotic mountain sheep and goats have been eliminated for food, as hunting trophies, or to make grazing room for domestic sheep and goats. Of course, snow leopards cannot distinguish between wild and domestic prey. Consequently they incur the wrath of their competing human neighbors. Despite a ghostly manner and mystical charms, the snow leopard cannot avoid the snare traps hidden on game trails.

As this imperilled cat teeters on the edge of extinction, the people also struggle to live in this unforgiving environment. Ways must be found to make the survival of the snow leopard economically viable to the humans. But poaching presents an almost irresistible temptation to these impoverished people. The demand for its fur and other body parts brings untold income to their struggling economies. Financing school and healthcare systems in communities that adopt protection measures and discourage poaching may be

The Snow Leopard

The snow leopard is an elusive and ghostly cat. It dwells within the realm of some of the earth's loftiest peaks. And when it appears, it seems to grace us with its mystical presence, magically appearing, as if it stepped off a cloud. A solitary hunter, living where the mountains nudge the heavens, it seems to be a bridge between this world and the spirit world. The snow leopard is the King of the Clouds.

The ancient shaman used the pelt of the snow leopard as a magic carpet, believing the soul of the leopard would carry them to a higher plane of consciousness. So did the Mongolian Lamaists, who incorporated the snow leopard's fur into their own traditions, placing pelts in the middle of a courtyard at the beginning of Tsam dances, the ancient religious dances of Mongolia, where the dancers wear magnificently ornamented costumes and elaborate masks. Even today, snow leopard pelts are rumored to cover the seats of expensive cars. Though coveted by man, the snow leopard's coat, with its dark spotted markings and rosettes, enables the leopard to vanish completely into its harsh environment. In his book *The Snow Leopard*, author Peter Matthiessen writes, 'The rarest and most beautiful of the great cats, the snow leopard … is wary and magical to a degree, and so well camouflaged in the places it chooses to live that one can stare at it from yards away and fail to see it.'

The fur of the snow leopard is whitish-grey tinged with yellow and is covered by dark open or indistinct rosettes and spots. The fur on the belly, chest and chin is close to pure white. The dense woolly under-fur allows the snow leopard to withstand the frigid temperatures in its mountain home.

Living high in mountains that are the rooftop of the world – the Himalayas, the Pamirs, the Karakorans, the Hindu Kush and the Tien Shan – this mighty cat is one of the few predators to view the world from above. They roam a one million square mile

(2,590,000 sq km) area in 12 ethnically diverse countries: Afghanistan, Bhutan, China, India, Kazakstan, Kyrgyz Republic, Mongolia, Nepal, Pakistan, Russia, Tajikistan and Uzbekistan.

The snow leopard's body is superbly designed for mountain predation. It has large snowshoe-like paws, short thick legs and well-developed chest muscles to aid in climbing steep mountain ledges. Its skull is flat across the top, with a deep notch down to a wide nose, allowing for larger nasal passages to breathe in the thin, cold mountain air. The snow leopard has the longest, thickest tail of all the cats, vital for balancing as it races up narrow game trails after its sure-footed prey, the mountain sheep and goats. The snow leopard stalks prey that is every bit as elusive and at home in the mountains as it is. Favorite prey include the legendary Marco Polo sheep, with one of the longest curled horns in the world; the markhor, with long spiralled horns; the ibex; Himalayan tahr, bharal sheep and several varieties of deer. However, the snow leopard is an opportunistic hunter who will also eat smaller gazelles, rabbit, marmot, and even the tiny pika.

Following the migration of their larger prey along the ridgelines, bluffs and cliffs can make eating a major uncertainty at times. Unfortunately, many of the exotic mountain sheep and goats have been eliminated for food, as hunting trophies, or to make grazing room for domestic sheep and goats. Of course, snow leopards cannot distinguish between wild and domestic prey. Consequently they incur the wrath of their competing human neighbors. Despite a ghostly manner and mystical charms, the snow leopard cannot avoid the snare traps hidden on game trails.

As this imperilled cat teeters on the edge of extinction, the people also struggle to live in this unforgiving environment. Ways must be found to make the survival of the snow leopard economically viable to the humans. But poaching presents an almost irresistible temptation to these impoverished people. The demand for its fur and other body parts brings untold income to their struggling economies. Financing school and healthcare systems in communities that adopt protection measures and discourage poaching may be the most efficient way to help the snow leopard. Although fully protected under the Endangered Species Act, enforcement of the laws is difficult in the remote areas that these high mountain predators inhabit.

While the snow leopard is classified as a big cat, it does not roar. The vocal folds are not as developed as in the other big cats – the lion, tiger, jaguar and leopard. Instead it lets out a hair-raising yowl. Centuries ago, people heard this scream and thought the mountains were possessed by ghosts, demons, or the legendary Yeti. Their scream allows solitary snow leopards to hear each other's mating calls, between January and March. Their calls must carry great distances in order to be heard by a potential suitor that could be up to 25 miles away. Scent marking also advertizes their presence to other snow

The snow leopard's tail is as long as its body.

leopards, alerting a potential mate that it is breeding season. Once snow leopards locate each other, they will greet with a quiet chuffing sound similar to that of the tiger. The pair will unite to hunt and mate frequently while the female is on heat.

When the time comes, the female will set out alone to give birth to from one to five tiny cubs. The gestation period is from 98 to 104 days. Born blind and helpless, they are totally dependent on their mother. Since they are born with all the spots they will ever have, the young cubs seem to wear a dark stripe down their spine, due to the closely clustered spots. As the cubs grow, the spots separate and become distinguishable. In their

Solitary animals, snow leopards live in large territories with males and females only coming together for a short while around the time of mating.

first winter they have the added protection of denser winter fur, against the unforgiving climate. The strained mother must not only feed herself, but now her young too. It will be a difficult time.

As the young venture out onto the ledges and ridges of their world, they must learn that danger can be found in loose rock, avalanches, and other predators. The eagle and the wolf are always looking for an easy meal. But meals are never easy in the wild. In order for the cubs to ultimately catch prey, they must first learn to pounce and bite. This comes to them instinctively through play and mock attacks with each other. But it only looks like fun play to us. To the young snow leopards, it is serious practice for their future profession, to be a great hunter. Without learning these lightening swift skills they will not live long.

At four to five months of age, the young follow their mother on hunts. They observe, yet often bungle her attempts with their over-exuberance. Everything they learn about stealth and patience in the hunt is from her. As they start the challenge of taking down swift prey, it is a dangerous time. The young do not yet possess the timing and coordination that their mother has. They could be kicked by sharp hooves or gored by horns or antlers. Life can be short for the young cubs. During their first year on their own they are especially vulnerable and not all survive to adulthood.

At 18 to 22 months of age, with their skills improving, the young adults venture far and wide to establish their own territories. With the problem of ever-shrinking habitat, it is daunting for them to compete with more mature snow leopards for the last remaining mountainsides. Much of the snow leopard's habitat is fragmented, making it uncertain whether they will find one another, affecting future genetic diversity. Biologists have seen evidence of snow leopards traveling through the lowlands of the southern Gobi region of Mongolia. Hot and desolate, it was thought impossible for the snow leopard to cross such terrain. Although not officially listed, many believe there are two subspecies already in existence; a main southern snow leopard, and a northern Mongolian/Russian snow leopard.

Not only are there uncertainties in finding a new territory to call home, a young snow leopard may find it empty of viable prey that it needs to survive. Several projects have been started to re-establish some of the lost prey herds. Along the Pakistan-China border, herders have been given financial incentives to protect the wildlife in the Khunjerab National Park, once a lambing ground for the wild Marco Polo sheep. Overgrazed by their domestic sheep, they have agreed to stop this practice, especially during the critical lambing season of Marco Polo sheep, which are the snow leopard's traditional prey. In the Bar Valley in northern Pakistan, a famous hunting region for ibex, natives agreed to stop hunting for three years to help re-establish the herds, and then only to hunt if they held a permit.

Survival depends not only on the skill of hunting scarce prey, but on careful footing on deadly precipitous cliffs. Additionally, the snow leopard must step cautiously to avoid snare traps placed along game trails by poachers. Garments of snow leopard fur were once highly prized, but worn only by the leaders of Asian nomadic tribes. During the height of the fur industry, however, thousands were taken, as eight to ten pelts were required to make one coat. In oriental medicine, snow leopard bones are used as a substitute for tiger bones, making the snow leopard skeleton also prized. Only by educating the next human generation can ancient practices be ended that are so lethal to this endangered cat.

The snow leopard illustrates the difficulty and delicacy of life. Perhaps the ancient shaman was right; they are indeed magical. This amazing cat has survived for centuries in the impenetrable mountains and valleys of Central Asia, enduring poaching, shrinking habitat and a brutally harsh environment. With yet more people and modern technology, the remote mountaintops are becoming increasingly accessible and crowded. Can we share the Himalayas with this mystical cat, or shall we only hear the tale of its lonely cries in the still mountain air?

The snow leopard's color and coat pattern provide perfect camouflage in its rocky habitat.

The Clouded Leopard

The clouded leopard is named after the large blotches on its sides, with dark borders and light interiors, which are said to resemble gathering storm clouds. To some, the dark markings look like the pattern found on the large ball python, a snake that shares the clouded leopard's habitat. These markings allow the clouded leopard to hide, patiently draped on a tree limb, in the dappled light of the dense jungle, waiting for unsuspecting prey. Living in the trees, this cat is the master of camouflage in the jungles of Borneo, Thailand, Bangladesh, Sumatra, and China.

Known as the Tree Tiger in Malaysia, the clouded leopard's coat is highly coveted. It was used as a ceremonial jacket in Taiwan, where the clouded leopard is now considered extinct. In the four sub-species, the color of the background fur ranges from ochre to tawny to silvery-grey. Its markings consist of large blotchy spots with dark borders on the flanks, black spots on the legs and shoulders, long black bands streaming out of the corner of the eyes, and thick bars of black around the neck.

Like many wild cats, not only is the fur prized, other parts are also illicitly sold. The most coveted are the distinctive large canines of the clouded leopard. In proportion to its body size, the clouded leopard has the longest canines of any of the felids. In fact, the teeth are very similar to those of the extinct saber-tooth tiger of North America, *Smilodon fatalis*. Pictures of saber-tooth tigers would lead us to believe the long canines of the clouded leopard hang outside the mouth. Amazingly, they fit inside and are not visible. Rather than looking like its fearsome ancestor, the clouded leopard instead has one of the most endearing faces of all the cats. No matter what it may look like, though, it is a capable predator, and those daggers allow it to take fairly large prey, such as deer, wild boar and primates.

The clouded leopard lives most of its life in trees where it both hunts and rests.

The stripes and blotches on the clouded leopard's coat provide
perfect camouflage in the dappled light of the rainforest.

The clouded leopard possesses characteristics of not only the big cats but also the small cats, seeming to be a bridge between the two with its intermediate size. It is in a genus all by itself, *Neofelis nebulosa*. It is similar to the small cats in the fact that it is a great climber. It rivals the margay of South America in its ability to race down a tree head first; most cats have to back down a tree, or jump out of it. What gives this cat this ability are its short stocky legs for climbing, a long tail for balance, sharp claws for clinging, and flexible ankles for rotation. It tightly wraps all four paws around a limb and hangs on. It can also hang and move on the underside of a branch and, like several of the smaller cats, it is capable of hanging from only its hind legs. This arboreal dexterity allows the clouded leopard to sneak up on monkeys, birds, and snakes living in the trees.

DNA studies have shown that the clouded leopard shares the same lineage as the big cats that roar, though it cannot roar. The vocalization of the clouded leopard consists of bird-like, high-pitched chirps, similar to many of the small cats and the cheetah. Like most cats they produce explosive growls and snarls when alarmed. Another sound the clouded leopard makes is unique to it, the tiger and the snow leopard. It is the 'prusten' or 'chuff'. It is a pronounced, friendly greeting in the tiger, but seldom heard in the snow leopard. All three cats physically push air through their lips to make the sound.

The eyes of the clouded leopard almost have the slit-like pupils characteristic of the small cats, rather than round ones like the bigger cats. When the larger felines close their pupils, they become small circles, similar to those in humans. The exception is the vertical oblong of the clouded leopard's eye, which is halfway between the circular pupil of the big cat and the vertical slit of a small cat.

What biologists know about the clouded leopard has come mostly from observation of animals in captivity. Despite this, the clouded leopard is hard to maintain in captivity because of the difficulty in breeding it. There is a high incidence of aggression between males and females, often resulting in the death of the smaller female. Much of the development in artificial insemination in wild felids grew out of a need to impregnate the female safely. However, this is a very expensive and time-consuming procedure that is not practical for all breeders. Present captive management techniques include introducing breeding pairs to each other at an early age, so they become bonded before sexual maturity, which occurs around two years of age.

After mating, a female can have one to five cubs in a litter, with two or three the norm. Cubs are fairly independent by ten months of age. Like the small cats they tend to develop more rapidly than the bigger cats, probably out of necessity. Cubs must develop fast; scampering up trees to hide while their mother is hunting. Their prey is smaller too, allowing young cats to hone their skills more quickly than their bigger cousins. Coordination and timing take longer to learn and are more critical in order to bring down a half tonne buffalo, rather than a small rodent.

The clouded leopard lives in a variety of habitats, from evergreen tropical rainforest to secondary logged forest, grassland and scrub. It has been reported in Myanmar and Thailand living in open, dry tropical forest. In Borneo it was found to inhabit mangrove swamps. Despite this variety of habitat, the clouded leopard is severely impacted by deforestation, as it lives in symbiosis with its prey. It is dependent on thick forest cover, and though it may be able to survive in areas less dense, the prey it is so dependent upon may not. Unfortunately, clear cutting rather than selective cutting is standard practice, causing great damage to tropical eco-systems.

The clouded leopard is also being eliminated by poachers, who profit from the demand for its teeth, pelt and bones, for ceremonial decoration and for medicinal purposes. More in-depth studies, in the wild, of this rare and stunning feline are needed, as a conservation policy is impossible without solid scientific knowledge of habits and habitat. Armed with newer knowledge, hopefully protection can be afforded these jungle masters, so only their coat will be considered cloudy, not their future.

Leopard Distribution

Stretching across Africa and Asia the range of the leopard is the greatest of all the big cats.

Clouded leopards range throughout the rain forests of South-East Asia while the snow leopard inhabits the mountainous regions of Central Asia.

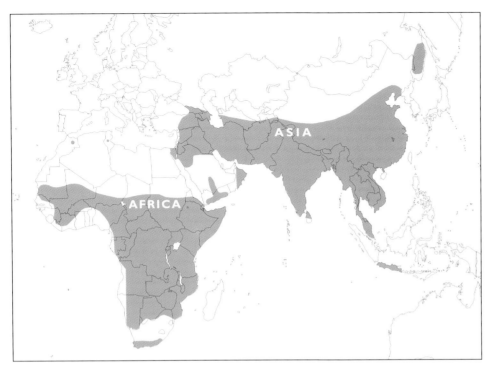

Leopards

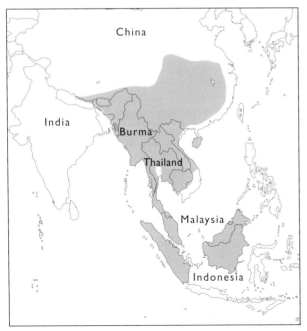

Clouded Leopards

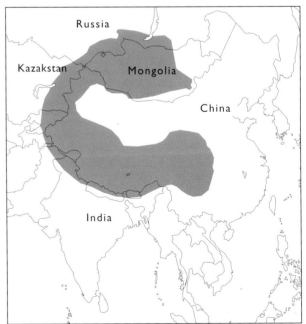

Snow Leopards

Leopard Facts

Scientific Name: *Panthera pardus*

Non-related species

    Snow Leopard   *Uncia uncia*

    Clouded Leopard   *Neofelis nebulosa*

Subspecies

In the past over 20 have been suggested, but of these a number, including the Zanzibar Leopard and the Caucasian Leopard are now considered extinct, but more significantly the 11 subspecies attributed to Africa may only be slight regional variations of a single subspecies. It may be that today there exist only eight separate subspecies which include:

Sri Lankan Leopard	*Panthera pardus kotiya*
North Chinese Leopard	*Panthera pardus japonensis*
Arabian Leopard	*Panthera pardus nimr*
Amur Leopard	*Panthera pardus orientalis*
Persian Leopard	*Panthera pardus saxicolor*

Weight: males   44-205lb (20-93kg)

                  females   37-99lb (17-45kg)

Body Size

Head and body length:	59-83in (150-210cm)
Tail length:	27-43in (68-110cm)
Shoulder height:	28-32in (71-81cm)

Females are typically 20% to 40% smaller than males

Life History

Independence:		18-24 months
Sexual maturity:	male	24-36 months
	female	33 months
Life expectancy:	wild	10-12 years
	captive	up to 23 years

In the wild approximately 50% of leopards perish before reaching maturity

Breeding Biology

Estrus:	46 days cycle, on heat 6-7 days
Gestation:	90-105 days
Number of cubs:	1-4, twins most common
Birth weight:	0.9-1.5lb (0.4-0.7kg)

Born blind and when young moved by mother about every 3 days for protection

Recommended Reading

Big Cat Diary: Leopard by Jonathan Scott, Angie Scott, Collins, 2003

A Time with Leopards by Dale Hancock, The Crowood Press, 2000

The Snow Leopard by Peter Matthiessen, Vintage, 1998

Index

Biographical Note

Cyndi Gamble has been editing and writing wildlife documentaries since her days working in television. As well as producing several feature films about exotic animals, Cyndi has raised, trained and filmed wolves, wolverines, coyotes and foxes. In 1992, Cyndi went into partnership with Craig Wagner to run the Center for Endangered Cats. Their feline ambassadors have graced books, magazines, newspapers, posters and calendars all over the world. They have traveled extensively across the USA, with their 'Great Cats of the World Show'; educating people about the problems cats are facing in the wild. Cyndi lives in Minnesota.

Rodney Griffiths is a nature photographer of international repute. He spends some three quarters of every year in far-flung corners of the globe studying and photographing his subjects. His work has been published in Europe, America and Japan in books, magazines, calendars and greetings cards. He and his images have appeared on television on the Discovery Channel. His work covers a wide range of topics including landscapes, birds and mammals, although he has specialized in eagles, baby mammals and his real passion, the cat family. Rodney lives with his wife, Christine, in Buckinghamshire, England.